DECORATIVE DETAILS
  of the 18th Century by W. & J. Pain

DETAILS DECORATIFS
  du 18e Siecle par W. & J. Pain

DETALLES DE DECORADO
  del Siglo XVIII por W. & J. Pain

DETAILS DECORATIFS

DU 18e SIECLE

par

WILLIAM & JAMES

PAIN

Préface de

Prof. A. E. RICHARDSON

DETALLES DE DECORADO

DEL SIGLO XVIII

por

WILLIAM & JAMES

PAIN

Prefacio del

Prof. A. E. RICHARDSON

DECORATIVE
DETAILS

OF THE EIGHTEENTH CENTURY
by
WILLIAM & JAMES
PAIN

with a preface
by
Prof. A. E. RICHARDSON

LONDON
A. TIRANTI
72 CHARLOTTE STREET, W.1

1946

PRINTED AND MADE IN GREAT BRITAIN BY
BARNARD & WESTWOOD LTD., LONDON, W.1

NO person in the annals of late eighteenth century architecture, not even the enterprising Robert Adam, did more to widen taste among the people than William Pain, who styles himself " Architect and Joiner." There were many such figures in England in those days whose names are forgotten, but whose works confront us wherever we turn. Yet it was William Pain who held first place in the popular esteem. Thus we feel interested in the publications which bear his name, perhaps because they provide an index to certain pleasant doorways and house fronts which we encounter in country towns and villages. Not that this modest architect's books were unknown in London, far from it, nor in Bristol, Dublin, or New York for that matter. It is, therefore, to his abiding glory and credit to have achieved so much by giving so freely, and so opportunely, when society was changing its make-up. This short essay does not pretend to be a character study of a particular craftsman; for not only does insufficiency of data make such a study impossible, but there is not even a portrait in oils or pencil to give an idea of his personality. It was therefore, through his numerous illustrated books that his teachings became popular with journeymen carpenters, bricklayers, masons, and all sorts of mechanics. In those distant times, every small builder owned a copy of one or the other of his published works. And those Schoolmasters and country surveyors who dabbled in building, to the indescribable benefit of the clergy, lesser gentry, and farmers, knew when, and how, to select appropriate details from the popular copy book. All this, of course, was done without due acknowledgment, for genius as we know is merely the art of taking pains. But even granting all this and much more, it is no easy task to track things down in order to place vernacular house building in its true relation to the more fashionable mansions of the time. Yet, notwithstanding certain obstacles, it is possible to attempt views which are approximately correct, and, therefore, of greater value than mere generalisations on the subject. To-day we have come to the reluctant conclusion that some aspects of past architecture possess a quality which we of to-day despair to attain. We view such exemplars with respect wherever we encounter them, and there are plenty such in City, Town, Village and Countryside.

As for America, the weatherboarded houses are legion, and the details, both without and within, bear the impress of Pain's copy book style. It is indeed a pity that we have no full length portrait of this worthy architect and joiner to which we can pay homage.

But we do know that he lived at a time when good taste prevailed, and that builders and their apprentices were less harassed by controls and regulations then, than they are to-day. In a word, William Pain was a fine old-fashioned type of John Bull; direct and upright, truly a man of parts, honest and confident, with just that amount of logic and desire to be considered respectable which appeals to every English speaking individual. You can judge all this from the way he arranged his exemplars and the mission he undertook to educate both workers and public. It was no small task to provide the scenic background for middle class society at a time when everybody aimed at being genteel! William, we learn from authentic accounts, begat a son called James, who in time assisted his father. In turn, James brought two sons into the world, these boys he named respectively James, and George Richard. In due course these young men were apprenticed to Mr. John Nash, working, no doubt, on the elevations for Regent Street, Highgate Archway, and other affairs. Then in time they blossomed forth on their own account, crossed St. George's Channel to Ireland and acted as Architects and Builders in the neighbourhood of Cork. In this way history is made and architectural traditions are extended. It is not, however, with the descendants of William Pain senior, that this account is concerned, but with the influence of a British worthy whose name was familiar in every builder's yard, in England at least, even if in America it was less popular and was sometimes confused with that of Tom Paine the political writer. And if we are deprived of reading exact details of William Pain's daily life, what does that signify; we can at least understand his reasons for wishing to benefit his fellow workers. It should be recalled that during the period of which we are hearing, the surest passport of an Architect to fame was to publish a book. In all probability William thought in these terms—had not the redoubtable James Gibbs produced such a work? Was there not Ware's Compleat Body of Architecture? And why did the Knight of the Polar Star deal so civilly with the art of which he was such a master? As for the two handsome volumes published by the ingenious architects from Edinburgh, were these to be considered a mere gratuitous gesture? These great and valuable treatises on the esoteric art were both expensive and difficult to obtain. You have only to refer to the lists of subscribers to realise how exclusive the latter were. Yet illustrated books accorded with the spirit of this age of elegance, and there was no bar to ordinary builders imitating their social betters. At least these or similar thoughts may have been indulged in by William Pain, and on such theories it can be assumed he acted. The result was that when his delightful copy books first appeared a new building vernacular spread with great rapidity. We are prone in these enlightened times to attribute all changes to bright and intellectual persons, forgetting the aptitude of ordinary folk to take charge of affairs when fate orders. Such was the case when his Sacred Majesty King George the Third had been on the throne for a short period. This was the time when the American Colonies were still thought to be loyal, it was, moreover, the epoch of brilliancy in all branches of the polite arts. Honest William Pain, Architect and Joiner, belonged to this period. He entered the lists of authorship to find architectural giants curling lips of scorn at what they considered to be petty interference. There was little professional etiquette in those days, and no rules of conduct to be observed. William Pain however, was fortunate in finding a public ready to take his teachings at face value, and a publisher ready to take risks. His first book " The Builder's Pocket Treasure," a small, octavo volume consisting of 49 plates, was published in 1763. This was in the nature of a try out. In 1774 he published " The Practical Builder " or " Workman's General Assistant." This book, although it flattered the large publication by Robert and James Adam, was, *de facto,* a challenge to their limited influence, for William Pain saw with remarkable clarity that the vast majority of builders were in need of an authentic copy book. In this regard it is permissible to quote from the preface of the first edition of Pain's important little book. He writes : —

" The very great Revolution (as I may say) which of late has so generally prevailed in the State of Architecture especially in the decorative and ornamental department, will evince the necessity and eminent Utility of this publication. That taste (so conspicuous in our modern buildings) which is vainly sought in any other practical treatise, the workman will here find illustrated in a great variety of useful and elegant examples."

" Honest William," as he came to be known, had a twofold purpose in view when he penned this preface: first there was the intended compliment to the skill of the Brothers Adam, secondly the objective was to convince his followers of the need for such a treatise. Whatever we may think of this work to-day, it remains William Pain's creation, and furthermore it stands for designs and details which are above fashion. Although he was, as he modestly states, a mere Architect and Joiner, he had the mind which could transmute and mould anew. There was no need in those days to search for originality, this was a quest left for the enthusiasts of the late nineteenth century, and our own time. This charmingly simple guide book shows new and vivacious ideas which derive from the spirit of the age rather than from close study of Adam's meticulous plates. It is, therefore, both useful and fascinating to analyse this Architect author's methods. We can follow the theories he adopted, catch the fancy of those for whom he published his book, and draw our own conclusions. He had the great advantage over the more renowned of his contemporaries in being free to dispense with classical references. He was in fact able to present mouldings en suite, and to draw details which would appeal to modest folk. Thus his recipients were never uncertain as to his meaning, for the illustrations like the text were easy to follow. It was in fact a test of his restraint that he pursued the middle course of a man who was a joiner at heart, and one moreover who knew how to frame things neatly . Thus William Pain avoided those pitfalls which awaited all tyros outside the charmed circle of the leaders of taste. He did not assume more than ordinary knowledge, and he left deep research to those more qualified in the eyes of the *bon ton* to undertake it abroad. We are privileged to-day to read the past as we like; and if we are gifted with seeing eyes a new zest is added to casual perambulation. We encounter the influence of William Pain almost everywhere. We find traces of his penetrating genius in all the regions of England. We see how he gave rulings for external doorways, cornices, bow windows, staircases, chair rails, and skirtings. We find his influence in East Anglia and in the remote West Country. We see it in the Northern Counties, and in Kent and Sussex. He seems to have been ubiquitous. Yet his was the silent autocratic method of book work. Study of this lesser branch of the building style of the late eighteenth century is of the greatest value to-day, especially when new interest is being taken in Georgian Architecture and craftsmanship. We are astonished at the taste of the middling people, no less than at the benefits occurring from graceful standardisation of details and ornament. Much as we admire the magnificence of great houses, and wander spellbound through galleries of chaste character, it is the smaller homes which appeal to our inmost thoughts. We are quick to recognise the beauty of simple work; and we understand from Pain's book how the details and designs fulfilled everything required of them.

It was not because William Pain was a great man that he achieved so much. His gifts were limited; but he was endowed with vision and saw clearly that the times needed the sort of book he had the mind to publish. The result was a compilation of diverse illustrations with descriptions clear cut and free from abstruse meaning. There can be no doubt that the truest explanation of the style of the lesser houses built in all parts of the kingdom, between 1774 and 1810, is to be found in the series of books published by William Pain. Well does the poet describe the growing streets, the brick boxes neatly sashed, and all the allurements of suburban retreats. It is, however, doubtful whether travellers by stage coach or post-chaise gave any thought at all to the " Architect and Joiner " who toiled so successfully behind the scenes. On the other hand if you refer to many of the local guide books to country towns, such as were published round about the eighteen hundreds, you will find references to certain " Handsome brick houses " in almost every one. You may be certain that the builders who designed them had recourse to Pain's " Practical Builder."

To have an opinion about English architecture of any period one must begin by getting down to the truth; and where is it to be found but by study from examples in the streets of Country towns or in the quiet corners of villages? To those willing to learn, all things present themselves : facts start up at every turn. You have only to study buildings and you have the key to the social customs of the age in which you are interested.

The fact that English craftsmanship reached such a relatively high standard during the later years of the Georgian era can be attributed in no small part to those books which the builders could obtain. But the main interest to be derived from the study of Old Copy Books is not entirely confined to their contents or to the period which saw their publication. The student will rediscover a great deal of useful knowledge concerning methods of working and assembling materials. Thus the experience of those students of literature, who revel in old and tried works, may also be the experience of modest designers who wish to know the meaning of quality.

A. E. RICHARDSON.

Personne, dans les annales de l'architecture du 18ème siècle, pas même l'entreprenant Robert Adam, ne fit plus pour développer le goût parmi la population, que William Pain qui s'intitule " Architecte et Menuisier." A cette époque, il y avait en Angleterre, de nombreuses figures de ce genre, dont les noms sont oubliés mais dont les œuvres nous confrontent de toute part. Ce fut, cependant, William Pain qui tint la première place dans l'estime populaire. Quand nous nous intéressons aux œuvres publiées qui portent son nom, c'est peut-être parce qu'elles nous fournissent un catalogue de certains porches agréables ou de façades que nous rencontrons dans les villages et les villes de province. Non pas que les livres de ce modeste architecte fussent inconnus à Londres ; bien au contraire, pas plus d'ailleurs qu'à Bristol, Dublin ou New York même. C'est donc tout à sa gloire et tout à son crédit d'avoir tant accompli en se donnant si librement et opportunément alors que la société changeait d'aspect.

Ce bref essai ne prétend pas être une étude de caractère d'un certain artisan ; car non seulement l'insuffisance de références rend cette étude impossible mais il n'existe même pas un portrait à l'huile ou au crayon qui puisse fournir une idée de sa personnalité. C'est donc seulement par ses nombreux livres illustrés que son enseignement devint populaire parmi les menuisiers, les briquetiers, maçons, et toutes sortes d'artisans. En ces temps lointains, chaque petit entrepreneur possédait un exemplaire de l'une ou l'autre de ses œuvres. Et les maîtres d'écoles et arpenteurs qui prenaient quelque intérêt dans la construction, au grand bénéfice du clergé, de la petite aristocratie et des fermiers, savaient quand et comment choisir dans son livre populaire, les détails appropriés. Tout cela, se faisait sans rendre dû hommage car le génie, comme nous le savons, n'est que l'art de prendre de la peine. Mais même en admettant tout cela, et plus encore, ce n'est pas tâche aisée de déceler les faits pour placer la construction de la maison courante à sa propre place par rapport à celle des maisons de plus grand style. Cependant en dépit de certains obstacles il est possible d'exposer des vues à peu près correctes et qui ont donc une plus grande valeur que de simples généralisations sur le sujet. Avec regret, nous sommes aujourd'hui arrivés à la conclusion que certains aspects de l'architecture du passé possédent une qualité qu'aujourd'hui nous n'avons pas l'espoir d'atteindre. Nous regardons ces exemples avec respect quand nous les rencontrons quelque part et il y en a de nombreux que se soit dans la cité, les villes, les villages ou la campagne.

En Amérique, les maisons-châlets sont légion, et les détails, à l'intérieur comme à l'extérieur, portent la marque du style des cahiers de Pain. Il est sans doute malheureux que nous n'ayons pas un portrait en pied de cet honorable architecte et menuisier auquel nous pourrions rendre hommage. Mais nous savons qu'il vivait à une époque à laquelle le bon goût prévalait et les constructeurs et leurs apprentis étaient moins harassés par les contrôles et les règlements qu'ils ne le sont à présent. En un mot, William Pain était un remarquable spécimen de John Bull vieux jeu, franc et droit, vraiment l'homme de l'emploi, honnête et sûr de lui-même, avec tout juste cette quantité de logique et ce désir d'être considéré respectable qui plaît à tout individu de langue anglaise. Vous pouvez juger de tout cela à la manière dont il arrangea ses exemples et à la mission qu'il entreprit d'éduquer à la fois, ouvriers et public. Ce n'était pas petite tâche que de fournir le décor à une société bourgeoise, à une époque où chacun s'efforçait d'être aristocratique.

William, nous apprenons de source authentique, eut un fils appelé James, qui plus tard devint son assistant. A son tour, James mit au monde deux garçons dont les noms respectifs étaient James et George Richard. Le temps venu, ces deux jeunes gens devinrent les apprentis de Mr. John Nash, travaillant sans doute aux plans de Regent Street, Highgate Archway et d'autres travaux. Puis, à leur tour, ils se lancèrent à leur compte, traversant le détroit de St. George pour l'Irlande où ils exercèrent comme architectes et constructeurs dans les environs de Cork. C'est de cette façon que l'histoire se fait et que les traditions architecturales se répandent.

Ce n'est pas, cependant, des descendants de William Pain l'Ancien, que ce bref essai s'occupe, mais de l'influence d'un notable britannique dont le nom était familier sur chaque chantier de construction, en Angleterre du moins, si toutefois il était moins populaire en Amérique où on le confondait parfois avec Tom Paine, l'auteur politique. Et s'il nous manque d'être à même de lire des détails exacts sur la vie quotidienne de William Pain, que nous importe? . . . car du moins nous pouvons comprendre ses raisons pour désirer rendre service à ses compagnons de travail. On doit se rappeler qu'à l'époque dont nous parlons, pour un architecte, le chemin le plus sûr vers la célébrité, était de publier un livre. En toute probabilité, William pensait de même . . . . Le redoutable James Gibb n'avait-il pas composé un ouvrage? N'y avait-il pas le "Manuel Complet d'Architecture" de Ware? . . . et pourquoi le "Chevalier de l'Etoile Polaire" traitait-il si courtoisement de l'Art duquel il était un grand maître? Devrait-on considérer les deux beaux volumes publiés par les ingénieux architectes d'Edinburgh comme un effort sans portée? Ces grands et précieux traités sur l'Art Esotérique étaient à la fois coûteux et difficiles à se procurer. Il suffit de se reporter aux listes de souscripteurs pour se rendre compte combien elles étaient exclusives. Cependant les livres illustrés étaient dans l'esprit de cet âge d'élégance, et il n'y avait pas de raisons pour empêcher les petits entrepreneurs d'imiter leurs confrères plus haut placés dans l'échelle sociale.

C'est de cette façon ou de façon semblable que William Pain a dû raisonner et l'on peut imaginer que c'est suivant ces lignes qu'il a dû agir. Le résultat fut que, depuis l'apparition de ses délicieux cahiers un nouveau langage dans l'art du bâtiment se répandit avec rapidité. Nous avons une tendance à notre époque de progrès, d'attribuer tout changement aux intellectuels brillants, et d'oublier que l'homme du commun peut prendre charge d'affaires quand le Destin en ordonne ainsi. Ce fut le cas quand sa Sainte Majesté le Roi George III avait occupé le trône pour une courte période de 14 ans. C'était l'époque à laquelle on croyait encore à la fidélité des Colonies d'Amérique, époque d'ailleurs brillante dans toutes les branches des Beaux Arts. "L'honnête" William Pain, "architecte et menuisier," appartient à cette période : son entrée sur la liste d'auteurs amena sur la lèvre des géants de l'architecture une moue de dédain pour ce qu'ils considéraient une méprisable ingérence. Il y avait peu d'étiquette professionnelle à cette époque et pas de règles de conduite à observer. William Pain eut la chance de trouver un public prêt à accepter son enseignement pour sa propre valeur, aussi bien qu'un éditeur préparé à prendre des risques. Son premier livre " Le Trésor de Poche du Constructeur," un petit in-octavo, renfermant quarante planches, fut publié en 1763. C'était en quelque sorte un ballon d'essai. En 1774, il publia " L'Entrepreneur Pratique" ou "Aide Complet de l'Artisan." Ce livre, bien que flattant la grande édition de Robert et James Adam était, en fait, un défi porté à leur influence limitée car William Pain avait vu très clairement que la grande majorité des constructeurs avaient besoin d'un authentique livre de modèles. A ce sujet, il est permis de citer ce passage de la préface de la première édition de l'important petit livre de Pain.

" La très grande Révolution (si j'ose dire) qui, récemment, a si généralement prévalu dans le Monde de l'Architecture et plus particulièrement dans les branches de la décoration et de l'ornement, expliquera la nécessité et l'éminente utilité de cette publication. Ce goût (si en évidence dans nos constructions modernes) que l'on cherche vainement dans n'importe quel traité pratique, l'artisan le trouvera ici, illustré par une grande variété d'exemples utiles et élégants."

" L'honnête William " comme il devint connu, avait en vue, un double but quand il écrivit cette préface : Premièrement, l'intention de rendre hommage à l'habileté des frères Adam; deuxièmement, le désir de convaincre ses lecteurs de la nécessité d'un traité de ce genre.

Quoi qu'on pense de cette œuvre de nos jours, elle reste la création de William Pain, et demeure représentative de modèles et de détails au-dessus de la question de mode. Bien qu'il fut, comme il le dit modestement, un simple " architecte et menuisier," il avait l'esprit qui peut transformer et refondre. Il n'y avait pas besoin à cette époque de s'efforcer d'être original; cette tâche fut laissée aux enthousiastes de la fin du 19 ème siècle et de nos jours.

Ce petit guide, simple et charmant, présente des idées vives et neuves qui découlent plutôt de l'esprit de l'époque que de l'étude attentive des planches détaillées d'Adam. Il est donc à la fois utile et très intéressant d'analyser les méthodes de cet architecte auteur. Nous pouvons suivre les méthodes qu'il adopta, capturer les aspirations de ceux pour qui il publia son livre et tirer nos propres conclusions. Il avait ce grand avantage sur ceux de ses contemporains plus renommés en ce qu'il était libre de se dispenser de références classiques. En fait, il lui était possible de présenter des ensembles de moulures et d'esquisser des détails qui pourraient convenir aux gens moyens. De cette façon, ceux qui suivaient ses directions n'étaient jamais incertains de ses desseins car ses illustrations de même que son texte étaient toujours facile à suivre. La meilleure preuve de sa sobriété fut qu'il sut garder le juste milieu d'un homme qui restait de cœur un menuisier et qui avait le don d'encadrer joliment. C'est pourquoi William Pain évita ces écueils qui menaçaient les novices en dehors du cercle magique des arbitres du goût. Il ne se flatta pas d'avoir plus que des connaissances ordinaires et laissa les recherches plus fouillées à ceux qui étaient plus qualifiés aux yeux de la mode pour les entreprendre . . . C'est aujourd'hui notre privilège de lire le passé comme nous l'entendons et si nous avons de bons yeux, un nouvel intérêt s'ajoute au hasard de nos promenades. Nous rencontrons presque partout l'influence de William Pain. Nous trouvons des traces de son génie pénétrant dans toutes les régions de l'Angleterre. Nous voyons comment il énonça des règles pour les portes extérieures, corniches, bow windows, escaliers, antebois et plinthes. Nous rencontrons son influence dans les comtés de l'Est et les coins perdus de l'Ouest. Nous la trouvons dans les comtés du Nord aussi bien que dans le Kent et le Sussex. Il paraît avoir le don d'ubiquité. Cependant sa méthode était la méthode livresque, silencieuse et autocratique.

L'étude des branches mineures du style de construction de la fin du 18 ème siècle est, de nos jours, de la plus grande valeur, particulièrement quand un nouvel intérêt est pris dans l'architecture et les œuvres d'art de la période des Georges. Nous sommes étonnés par le goût des gens moyens non moins que par les bénéfices résultant de la gracieuse standardisation des détails et des ornements. Autant que nous admirions la magnificence des grands édifices et bien que nous errions, muets d'admiration, au travers de galleries de sobre caractère, il n'en reste pas moins que ce sont les intérieurs plus modestes qui au fond, nous plaisent le mieux. Nous sommes prompts à reconnaître la beauté d'une œuvre simple et nous comprenons, dans le livre de Pain, que ses détails et ses dessins satisfont pleinement ce qu'on attend d'eux.

Ce n'est pas parce que Pain était un grand homme qu'il fit tant. Ses dons étaient limités : mais il avait le don de vision et il vit clairement que son temps avait besoin du livre qu'il avait envie de publier. Le résultat fut une compilation d'illustrations diverses accompagnées de descriptions claires et dépourvues de toute .obscurité. Il n'y a pas de doute que la plus véridique explication du style des maisons de moindre importance bâties dans toutes les parties du Royaume entre 1774 et 1810, se trouve dans la série de livres publiés par William Pain.

Le poète décrit fort bien le développement de la rue, les boîtes de briques, joliment encadrées, et les attraits des retraites suburbaines. Il est cependant douteux que les voyageurs, en diligence ou en chaise-poste, aient accordé la moindre pensée à l'architecte-menuisier" qui travaillait avec tant de succès derrière la scène. D'autre part, si l'on se reporte à quelques-uns des guides locaux de villes de province, comme ceux qui se publiaient aux environs de 1800, on y trouve mentionné dans presque tous " Belles maisons de briques." Vous pouvez être sûrs que les entrepreneurs qui en ont fait les plans se sont aidés du " Constructeur Pratique " de Pain.

Pour avoir une opinion sur l'architecture anglaise de n'importe quelle période, il faut commencer par chercher la vérité ; et où peut-on la trouver, sinon par l'étude d'exemples dans les rues des villes de province ou les coins tranquilles des villages? A ceux désireux de s'instruire, toutes choses se présentent ; les faits jaillissent à chaque tournant. Vous n'avez qu'à étudier les bâtiments et vous avez la clef des usages sociaux de la période à laquelle vous vous intéressez.

Le fait que l'habileté professionnelle anglaise atteint un niveau relativement si haut pendant les dernières années de la période des Georges peut être attribuée en grande partie à ces livres que les entrepreneurs pouvaient obtenir. Mais l'intérêt principal que l'on dérive de l'étude de vieux traités n'est pas entièrement confiné à leur contenu ou à la période qui vit leur publication. L'étudiant découvrira de nouveau une grande quantité de connaissances utiles concernant le travail et l'assemblage des matériaux. Ainsi donc l'expérience des étudiants de littérature qui se plaisent à la lecture d'ouvrages anciens et éprouvés peut être aussi l'expérience des dessinateurs modestes qui désirent connaître la signification de " qualité."

A. E. RICHARDSON.

En los anales de la arquitectura de fines del siglo dieciocho, no hubo nadie, ni el emprendedor Roberto Adam, que hiciera más para ensanchar el discernimiento entre el pueblo, que hizo Guillermo Pain, el que a sí mismo se intitulaba " Arquitecto y Ensamblador." Por aquellos tiempos habia en Inglaterra muchas tales figuras cuyos nombres se han olvidado, pero cuyas obras encontramos hoy por doquiera que vayamos. Y sin embargo, fué Guillermo Pain el que alcanzó la cumbre de la estima popular. Por eso es que nos sentimos interesados en las publicaciones que llevan su nombre, debido quizá, a que ellas nos proveen un índice de simpáticas portaladas y fachadas, ésas que tanto abundan en pueblos y ciudades de provincia.

No quiere decir esto, que los libros de este modesto arquitecto fuesen desconocidos en Londres, nada de eso, pues Bristol, Dublin y hasta Nueva York los conocía. Su gloria y crédito perennes lo constituyen haber alcanzado tanto, produciendo tanto y tan oportunamente, en tiempos en que la sociedad estaba en continua evolución.

No pretende este corto ensayo ser un estudio del carácter de un artífice cualquiera, pues no solo resulta imposible por la falta de detalles suficientes, sinó, que no existe ni siquiera un retrato al óleo, ni bosquejo a lápiz que nos pueda dar idea de su personalidad.

Sabemos sin embargo, que con sus numerosos libros ilustrados, sus enseñanzas se hicieron populares entre los trabajadores, carpinteros, aljañiles y toda clase de jornaleros. En aquellos distantes tiempos, no habia ningún pequeño constructor que no tuviese alguno de los libros que habia publicado. Todos aquellos maestros de escuela y topógrafos provincianos que se metían a constructores, para indescriptible beneficio de clérigos, hidalgos y labradores acomodados, sabían perfectamente cuándo y cómo escoger detalles apropiados en el libro popular. Todo esto se hacía, naturalmente, sin pedir permiso alguno, pues el genio, como sabemos, consiste simplemente en el arte de tomarse el trabajo. Pero aun dando, todo esto, y mucho más por concedido, no resulta tarea fácil seguir la pista hasta poder llegar a colocar la construcción vernácula en su verdadera situación con relación a los más modernos edificios de la época.

Sin embargo, a pesar de ciertos obstáculos, todavía es posible emitir pareceres, correctos por aproximación y por lo tanto de mayor valor que generalizaciones sobre el asunto. Hoy dia tenemos que admitir, a pesar nuestro, que algunos aspectos de la arquitectura pasada están dotados de una calidad que nosotros, los de hoy, estamos lejos de alcanzar. Tales ejemplos, donde quiera que los hallamos, merecen nuestro respeto y en verdad no faltan casos, tanto en ciudad, como en villa, pueblo o aldea.

En lo que concierne a Norte América, los ejemplos de casas solapadas son innumerables, y sus detalles, tanto fuera como dentro, llevan impreso el sello del libro de Pain. Es una verdadera lástima que no tengamos un retrato de cuerpo entero de tan notable arquitecto y ensalmador, al que pudieramos hacer debido honor. Lo que sí sabemos es, que vivió en un tiempo cuando el buen gusto era general, y que entonces, tanto los constructores como sus aprendices estaban menos apremiados con reglamentos y restricciones que están los de hoy. En una palabra, Guillermo Pain fué un expléndido ejemplo de JOHN BULL enchapado a la antigua, tieso y derecho, un hombre de buenas cualidades, formal y confiado, que peseía esa lógica y deseo de ser considerado un hombre decente, que tanto saben apreciar todos los que pertenecen a la raza inglesa.

Uno puede juzgar esto, por el modo en que erregló sus ejemplares y la misión que se propuso, de educar tanto al obrero como al pueblo.

No era fácil tarea crear un fondo escénico para una sociedad de clase media en una época en que todo el mundo se esforzaba por parecer elegante!

Guillermo tuvo un hijo, llamado Jaime, según relación auténtica, y éste, en su tiempo, asistió a su padre. Jaime, luego, tuvo dos hijos que llevaron los nombres de Jaime y Jorge Ricardo. Estos dos jóvenes recibieron en su dia, aprendizaje con Juan Nash, trabajando sin duda en la elevación de Regent Street, Highgate Archway y otros lugares. Más adelante, florecieron éstos, por su propia cuenta, y cruzaron el Canal de San Jorge a Irlanda, estableciéndose como arquitectos y constructores en las cercanías de Cork. Asi se escribe la historia y se extiende la tradición de la arquitectura.

No concierne, sin embargo, a este pequeño ensayo, describir los descendientes de Guillermo Pain, sinó la influencia que ejerció un inglés notable cuyo nombre era en su dia familiar en todos los depositos de materiales de construcción, por lo menos en Inglaterra, pues si en Norte América era menos popular, se debia ello a que le confundían con Tom Paine, un escritor político.

Si como es verdad, no podemos leer detalles exactos de la vida normal de Guillermo Pain, eso no significa que no podamos al menos comprender las razones que tenía para desear beneficiar a sus compañeros de trabajo. Es necesario recordar que durante el período a que nos referimos, el pasaporte más seguro de un arquitecto para la fama, era el publicar un libro. Es muy probable que Guillermo pensase lo mismo; ¿ no lo habia hecho el famoso Jaime Gibbs? ¿ No existía ya un COMPLEAT BODY OF ARCHITECTURE, por Ware ? y ¿ por qué trataba tan cortésmente el Caballero de la Estrella Polar, el arte en que él era tan maestro ?

Pues qué diremos de los dos magníficos tomos publicados por los ingeniosos arquitectos de Edinburgo, ¿ Se tendrían que considerar estos libros como un gesto injustificado? Estos grandes y valiosos tratados sobre el arte exótico eran tan caros como difíciles de obtener. Solo hay que fijarse en las listas de subscriptores para ver cuán exclusivos eran éstos. Los libros ilustrados armonizaban con el espíritu de esta edad elegante y no se ponía obstáculo a que los constructores ordinarios imitasen a sus superiores en la escala social. Por lo menos, bien puede decirse que éstos o parecidos pensamientos son los que tendria Guillermo Pain y lógico es asumir que él llevase tales teorías a la práctica. El resultado fué, que cuando se dieron a luz sus deliciosos cuadernos, se extendió rápidamente un nuevo vocabulario de constructores.

En estos dias de luces, nos sentimos siempre inclinados a atribuir todos los cambios a notables e intelígentes personajes, pero nos olvidamos de la aptitud de gente ordinaria para hacerse cargo de los negocios, cuando el Destino lo ordena. Tal era el caso cuando su Inmensa Majestad, el Rey Jorge Tercero habia estado en el trono por el corto período de catorce años.

Por estos tiempos era cuando se creía que las Colonias americanas eran leales aún, además, era la época de brillantez en todas las ramas de la cortesía. El probo Guillermo Pain, arquitecto y ensalmador, perteneció a dicho período.

Al entrar en las listas de autores, se encontró con los gigantes de la Arquitectura, apucherando los labios con desprecio, por lo que ellos consideraban una intrusión descarada. En aquellós dias habia muy poca etiqueta profesional y ninguna regla sobre la conducta que se debería observar. Suerte tuvo Guillermo Pain en encontrar un público dispuesto a aceptar sus enseñanzas, tal y como se le daban, y un editor inclinado a correr riesgos.

El primer libro, *El Tesoro de bolsillo del Constructor,* un pequeño tomo en octavo con 49 laminas, fué publicado en 1763. Se strataba de una especie de prueba. En 1774 publicó "El Constructor Práctico" o "Ayuda General del Obrero." Este libro, aunque halagaba la publicación mayor de Roberto y de Jaime Adam, era " de facto " un reto a su limitada influencia, pues Guillermo Pain podía ver con extraordinaria claridad que la inmensa mayoría de constructores, necesitaba un cuaderno auténtico. En este respecto, nos es permitido citar del prefacio a la primera edición del importante librito de Pain, lo que escribe, dice asi :

"La grandísima revolución (como yo considero) que en estos últimos tiempos ha sido tan general en el Estado de Arquitectura y especialmente en las secciones de Decorado y Ornamento, demostrará la necesidad y eminente utilidad de esta publicación.

Ese gusto (tan conspícuo en nuestros modernos edificios) que en vano se busca en cualquier otro Tratado práctico, aquí lo encontrará el obrero ilustrado, en gran variedad de útiles y elegantes ejemplos."

El honrado Guillermo, como asi llegó a conocérsele, al escribir ese prefacio tenía dos objetos en vista ; allí estaba el encomio a la destreza de los hermanos Adam ; el segundo objetivo era convencer a sus propios admiradores de la necesidad de tal tratado. Lo que hoy podamos pensar de esa obra no importa, lo cierto es que es la creación de Guillermo Pain y además aboga por diseños y detalles que están sobre la moda.

Aunque él era, como modestamente se describe, un mero arquitecto y ensamblador, poseía una inteligencia capaz de transmutar y moldear de nuevo. En aquellos dias, no habia necesidad de andar buscando originalidad, esa busca, fué dejada para los entusiastas de fines del siglo diecinueve y los de nuestros propios dias.

Esta preciosa y simple guía nos presenta nuevas y vivaces ideas que se derivan del espíritu de la época, más que de concentrado estudio de las meticulosas láminas de Adam. Es pues, útil y fascinador analizar el tecnicismo de este autor arquitecto. Uno puede seguir las teorías que adoptó, cautivar la fantasía de aquellos para quienes publicó el libro y luego, venir a nuestras propias conclusiones. Poseía la gran ventaja sobre sus famosos contemporáneos, de estar libre de tener que acudir a referencias clásicas. Tanto es asi, que podia presentar, seguidamente, cualquier moldura y dibujar detalles que gustasen a la gente del pueblo. A eso se debia que sus adeptos no tuvieran nunca duda de su verdadera intención, pues sus ilustraciones, como su texto, eran fáciles de seguir. En verdad, la prueba de su propio freno era la de que siendo él, en realidad, un ensamblador por inclinación, supo adoptar un curso medio entre éste y otro que sabe hacer las cosas pulcramente. Por esa razón, Guillermo Pain supo evitar las trampas que esperaban a los novatos que no pertenecian al circulo mágico de los lider del gusto.

No pretendió tener más conocimientos que los que tenía ; a aquellos que en ojos del buen tono estaban mejor calificados que él, les dejó la tarea de hacer investigaciones por todas partes. Hoy tenemos el privilegio de leer el pasado como queramos ; si poseemos el don de tener ojos que ven, hallaremos un nuevo deleite en nuestra excursión fortuita. La influencia de Guillermo Pain, la encontramos por dondequiera. En todas las regiones de Inglaterra nos encontramos trazas de su ingenio. Vemos como dió reglas para pórticos externos, cornisas, miradores, balaustradas y zócalos. Vemos su influencia en la Anglia Este y la vemos en el remoto País Oeste. La hallamos en los condados del Norte y en los de Kent y Sussex, en el Sur. Parece como si hubiera estado siempre presente en todas partes ; y sin embargo, su método autocrático era el silencioso del trabajo de libro.

El estudio de esta sección menos importante del estilo de construcción de fines del siglo diecicocho, es hoy de un valor importantísimo, por volver el interés en la arquitectura y el arte georgianos. Nos asombra el gusto de la clase media no menos que los beneficios que se acumulan por la unificación graciosa de detalles y ornamento.

Por mucho que admiremos la magnificiencia de las grandes casas y vaguemos llenos de asombro por galerias de puro carácter, son los hogares modestos los que hacen más mella en nuestros pensamientos. Somos rápidos en reconocer la belleza de la obra sencilla, y con el libro de Pain podemos comprender como llenaron su cometido todos los detalles y diseños, dando de sí todo lo que se esperaba de ellos.

Que Guillermo Pain alcanzase tanto, no se debió a que fuese un sabio. Sus dones eran limitados, pero habia sido favorecido con una visión clara y previó que sus tiempos necesitaban precisamente el libro que él pensaba publicar. El resultado fué una compilación de diversas ilustraciones con descripciones claras y del todo libres de obtusa comprensión. No puede haber la menor duda de que la explicación más verdadera del estilo de las casas menos importantes edificadas por todas las partes del reino, entre los años 1774 y 1810, se puede encontrar en la serie de libros publicados por Guillermo Pain. Bien lo describe el poeta : la creciente calle, los cajones de ladrillo con sus delicados ventanales y todos los attractivos de los retiros suburbianos.

Es sin embargo dudoso, que ningún viajero de Diligencia o silla de posta ni siquiera pensara en el " Arquitecto y Ensamblador" que con tanto éxito trabajaba detrás de las escenas. Por otro lado, si uno consulta cualquier guía de ciudades provincianas, de aquellas que se publicaron hacia los mil ochocientos, se encontrará en casi todas ellas referencia a ciertas " preciosas casas de ladrillo." Bien puede uno estar seguro de que los constructores que las hicieron fueron guiados por el "Constructor Práctico," de Pain.

Para poder formar opinión sobre la arquitectura inglesa de cualquier período, tendrá que comenzar por la verdad, y ¿ dónde la podremos encontrar, si no es en el estudio de los ejemplares que existen en las calles de ciudades de provincia o en las esquinas de tranquilos pueblos? Para los que quieren aprender, todo sale a la mano y los hechos aparecen a cada paso. Solo tiene uno que estudiar edificios para obtener la clave de las costubres de la sociedad que le interesa.

El hecho de que el artífice inglés, llegó a un grado tan relativamente alto, durante los últmos años de la era Georgiana, puede atribuirse, en muy buena parte, a esos libros que el constructor podía conseguir. Pero el interés principal que se deriva del estudio de antiguos cuadernos, no se confina enteramente al contenido de ellos o el período en que se publicaron. El estudiante volverá a descubrir bastantes conocimientos útiles sobre los métodos de trabajar y el montaje de los materiales. Así, la experiencia de estos estudiantes de litera-tura que se deleitan con antiguas y probadas obras, podrá también ser la de humildes delineadores que deseen saber lo que significa calidad.

A. E. Richardson.

INDEX

Woodman & Mutlow sc.

2   3   4   5   6   7   8 ft.

1

W. & J. Pain del.

1   2   3   4   5

2

b

2 d

45

45

30

30

11 parts, each equal to 1 Diameter

30

1 d

d

a

c

e

10

2½

3 „ 6

8 D. 25 m.
5 Modillions.

12 9 6 3 0   1   2   3   4   5   6 f.t

3

Doric *d* Front.

b

a

c

e

11 Diam.

7 Diam: 3 min.
6 Modillions from Center to Center of Column.

45

40 35

12 Parts each part 1 Diameter.

3 8

6 D. 12 m.

12 Modillions

12 9 6 3 0   1   2   3   4   5   6 et

Ionic . Front .

6 Diam: 43 min.'
13 Modillions from Center to Center of Column.

6

48
37
2 d
35

70 m

13 parts each part 1 Diameter

30
1 d

3 — 6

6 D. 25m.
11 Modillions.
7 Diameters, 12 Modillions.

12 9 6 3 0   1   2   3   4   5   6

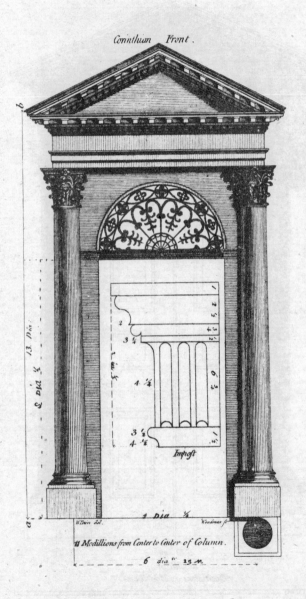

Corinthian Front.

Impost

Wtown del.   *Woodman fc*

4 DIA ½

11 *Medillions from Center to Center of Column.*

6 dia ¹⁵ 25 m.

8

5 in.

11'.8

3 .. 7

Russell Sculp. Nº9 Constitution Row.

Grays Inn Lane.

12 9 8 3 0   1   2   3   4   5   6

e

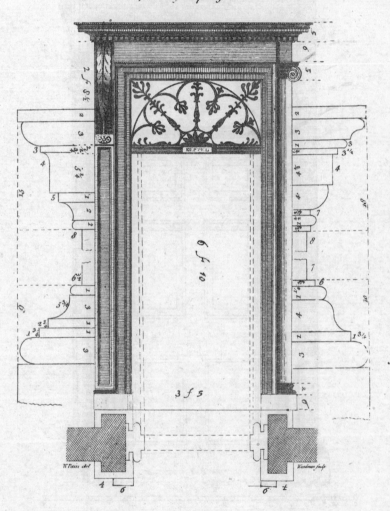

Frontispeice for out fide front,
or it may be ufed within
by omiting the fanlight.

Inside door and Dressing.

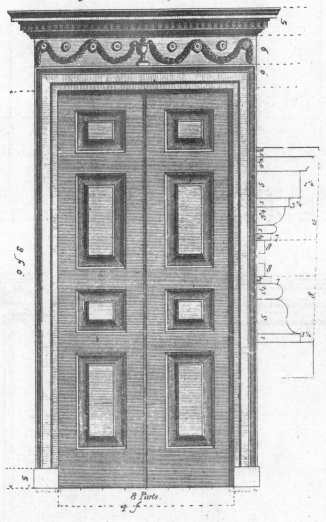

8 Parts.

11

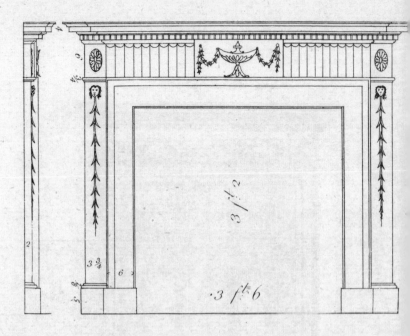

3 f.t 2

3 3/4

6

·3 f.t 6

2

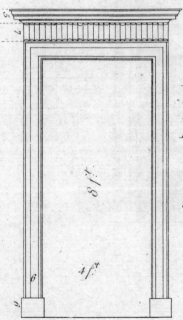

8 f.t

6

4 f.t

Architraves to Doors and Chim-
-neys, one Eighth, or one Ninth
of the Clear opening the Side
Pilaster ⅔ of Ditto; the Frieze
one ¼ of the Architrave, the Cornice
¾ of ditto; the Doors ³/8 of an Inch
to a Foot, the Chimneys ¾ of an Inch
to a Foot.

5½

Wm Pain delin.^t

Woodman & Mutlow Sculp.^t

13

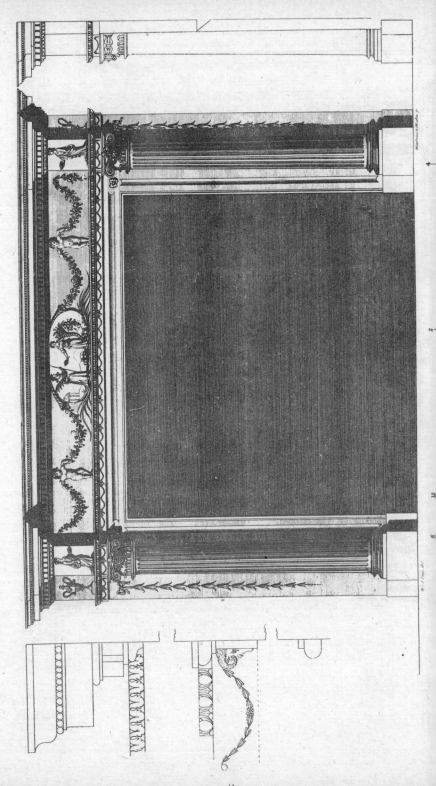

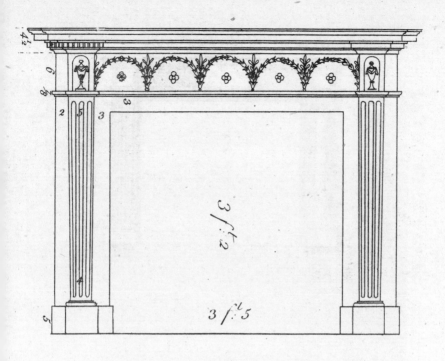

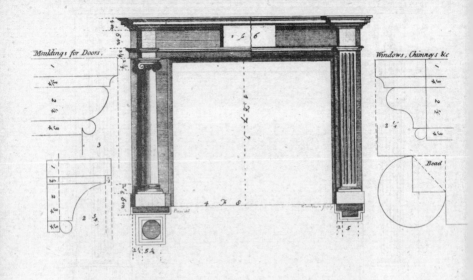

Mouldings for Doors.

Windows, Chimneys &c.

Bead

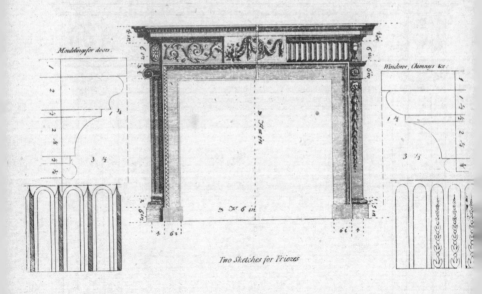

Mouldings for doors.

Windows, Chimneys &c.

Two Sketches for Triezes

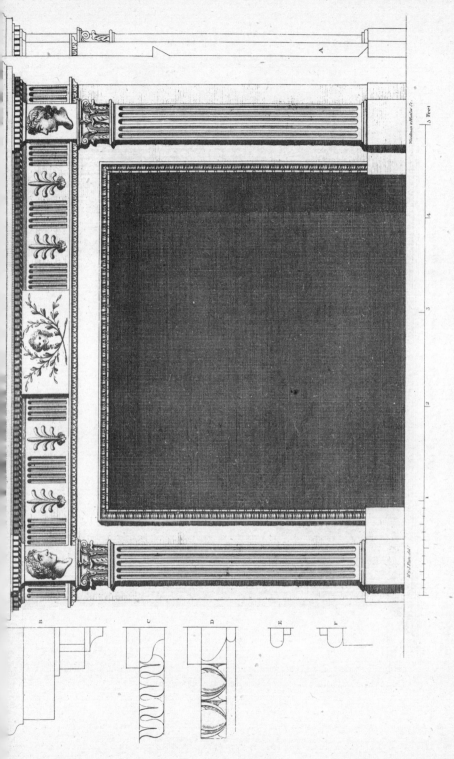

A

5 Feet
4
3
2
1

Woodman & Mutlow sc.

W^m I Pain del.

B   C   D   E   F

17

Design for a Chimney Peice, drawn one inch to a foot.

J.Royal Sculp.

18

19

5 Feet

20

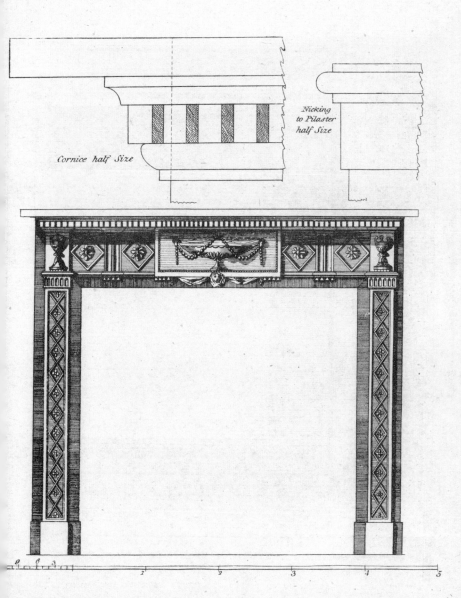

Cornice half Size

Nicking
to Pilaster
half Size

21

Chimney piece drawn one inch to a Foot

24

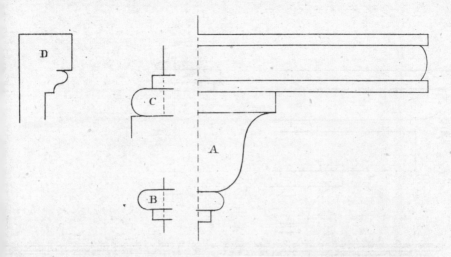

D

C

A

B

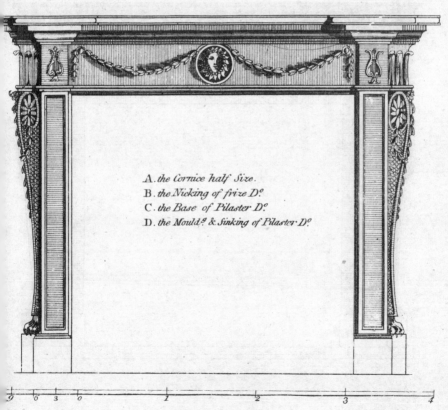

A. the Cornice half Size.
B. the Nicking of frize D.º
C. the Base of Pilaster D.º
D. the Mould.º & Sinking of Pilaster D.º

9   6   3   0   1   2   3   4

25

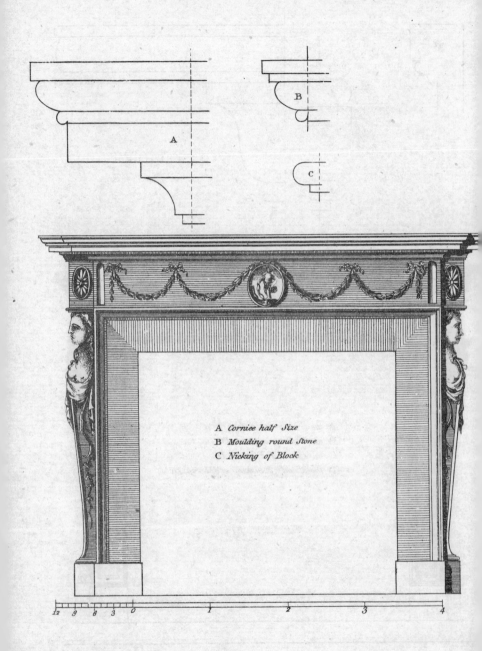

A *Cornice half Size*
B *Moulding round Stone*
C *Nicking of Block*

W.R.J.Rose del.

Wickham & Madden, Sculp. Barlow St.

5 feet

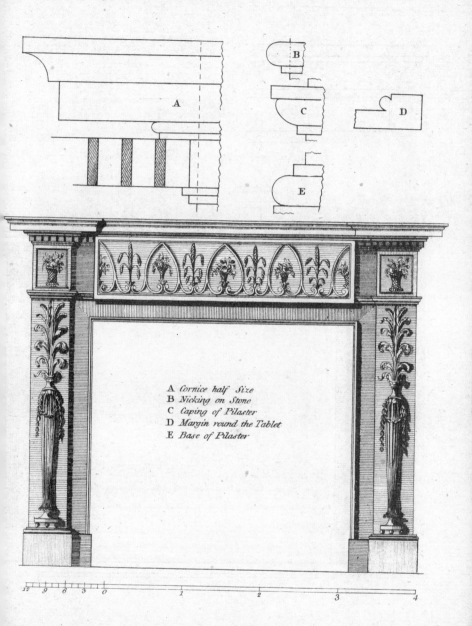

A *Cornice half Size*
B *Nicking on Stone*
C *Caping of Pilaster*
D *Margin round the Tablet*
E *Base of Pilaster*

29

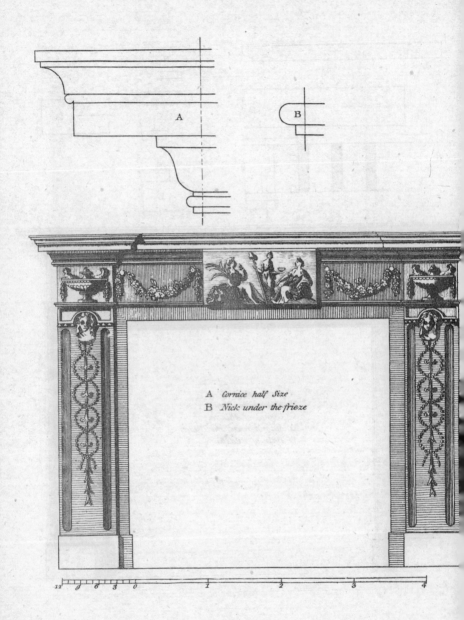

A   *Cornice half Size*
B   *Nick under the frieze*

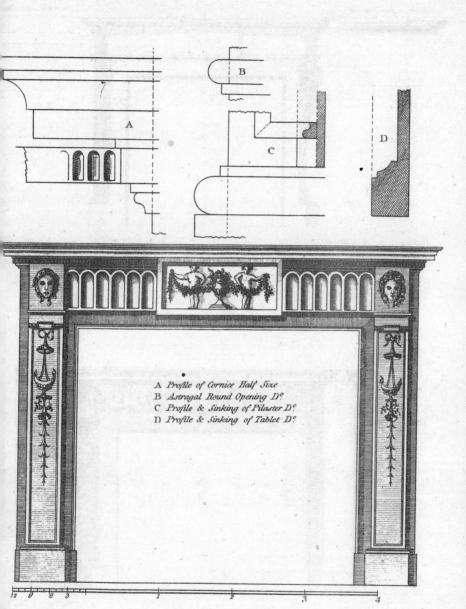

A *Profile of Cornice Half Size*
B *Astragal Round Opening D?*
C *Profile & Sinking of Pilaster D?*
D *Profile & Sinking of Tablet D?*

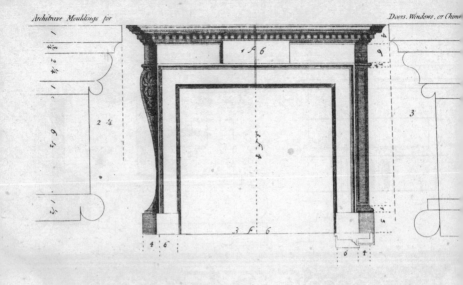

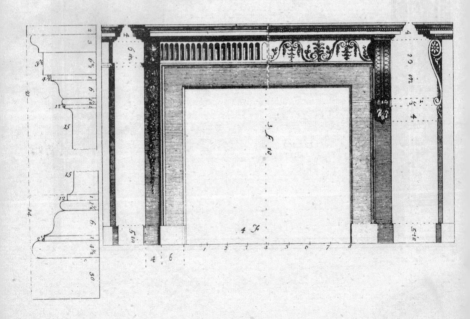

10 Inches, or 1 F.t

Two Designs for triglyphs figured full size for practice

from 1 foot 6 to 2 feet

3 Inches or 4.   4 or 4½ Inches.   3 In. or 4   4 or 4½ In.

33

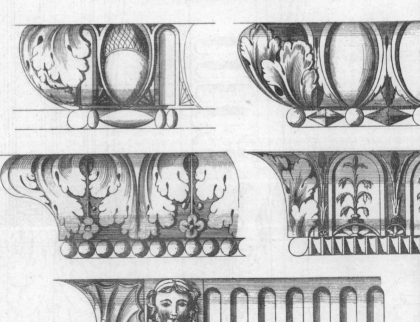

Seven or Nine Flutes between the Heads.

34

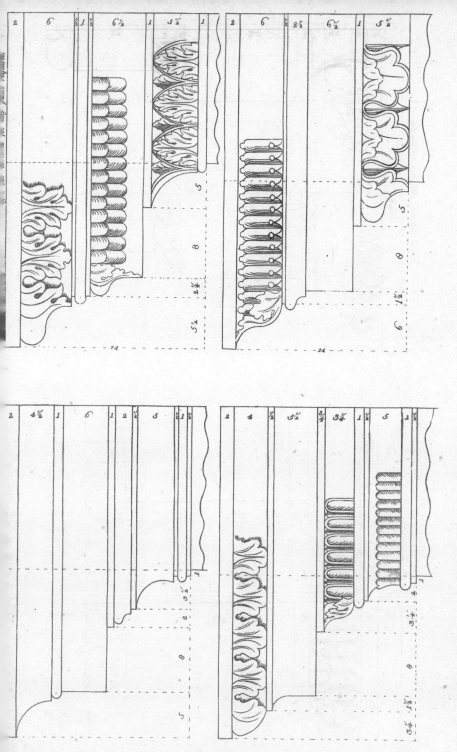

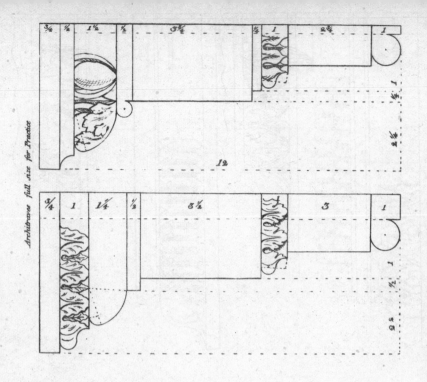

Architraves full size for Practice

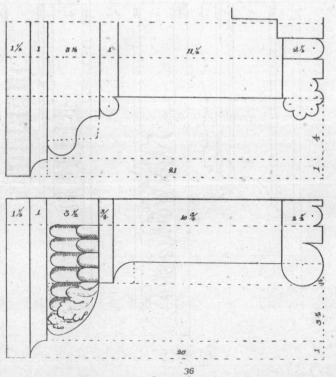

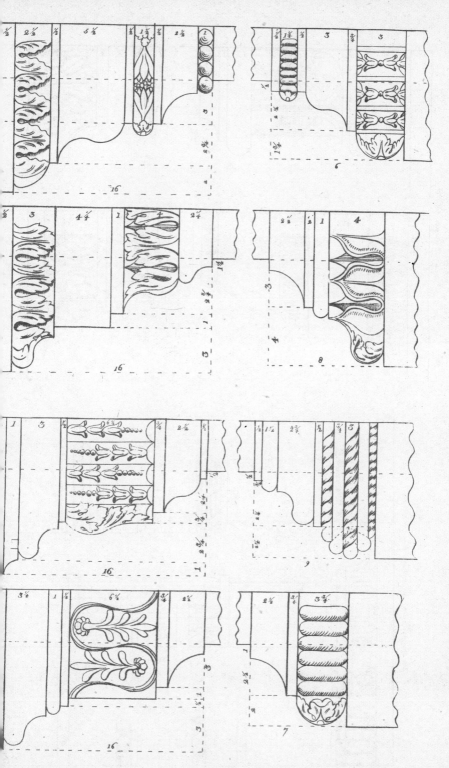

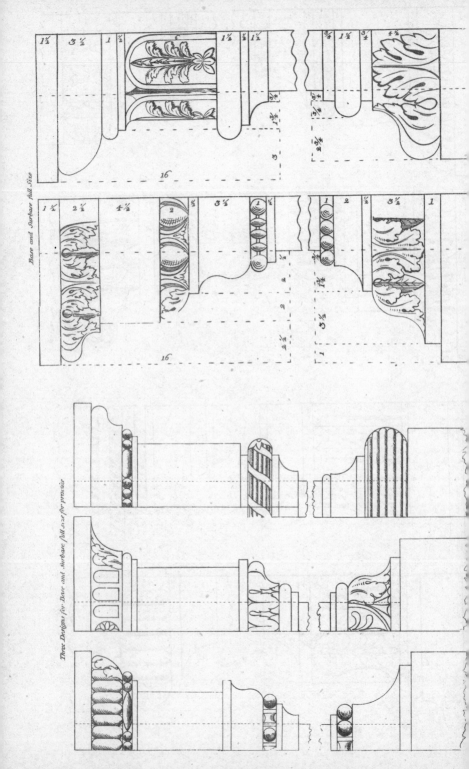

Base and Surbase full Size

Three Designs for Base and Surbase full size for portico

38

Four Designs for Surbase full size for practice.

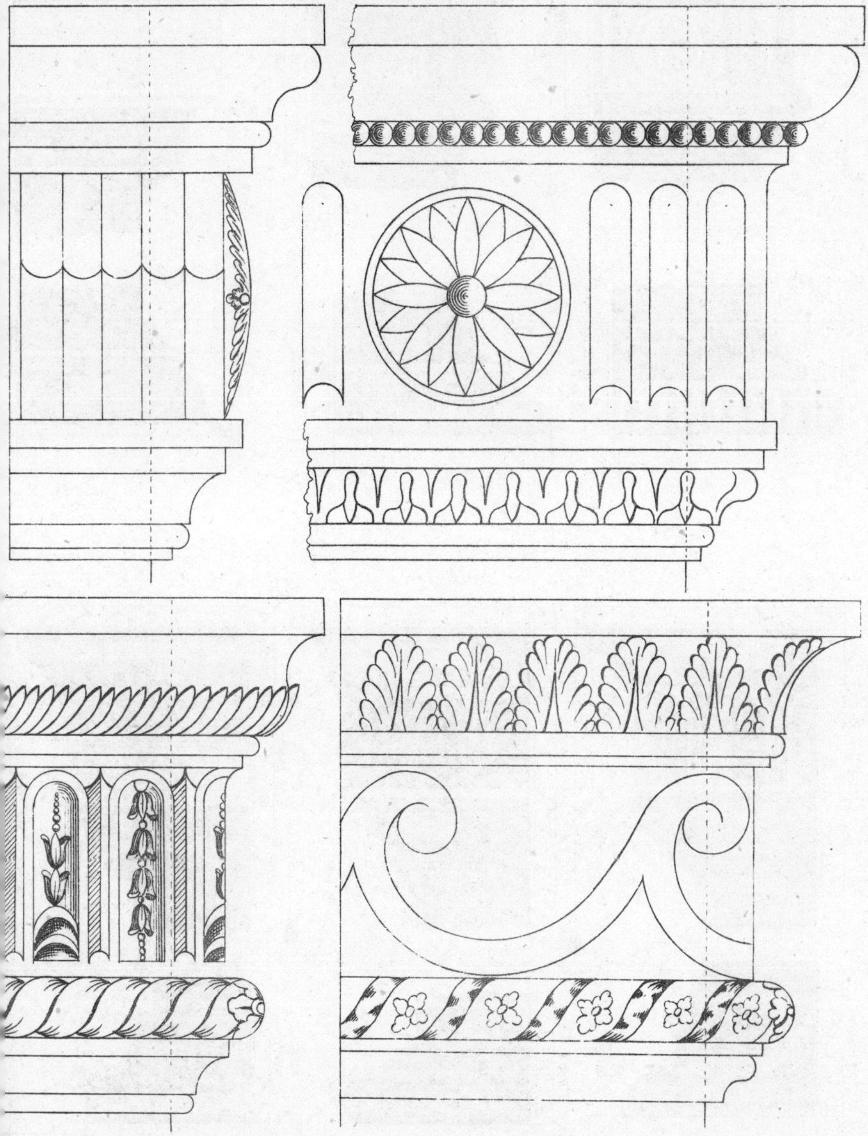

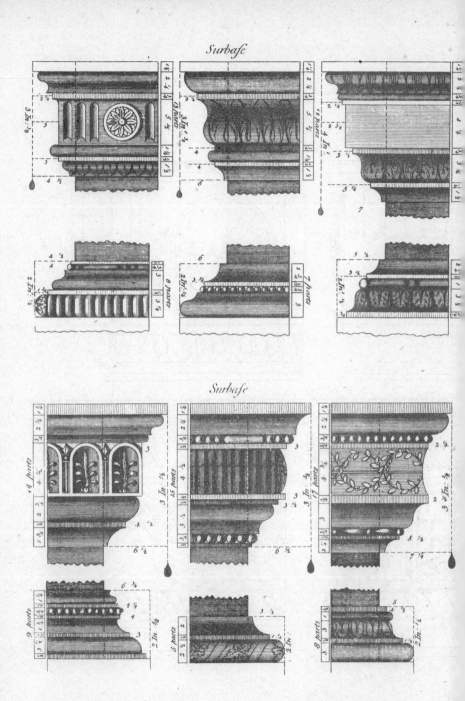

Surbase

Surbase

O4

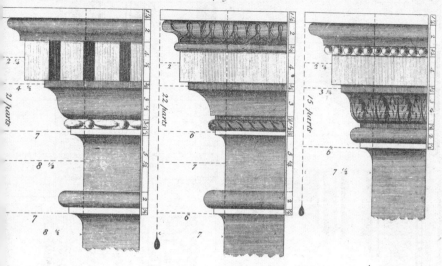

21 parts

22 parts

15 parts

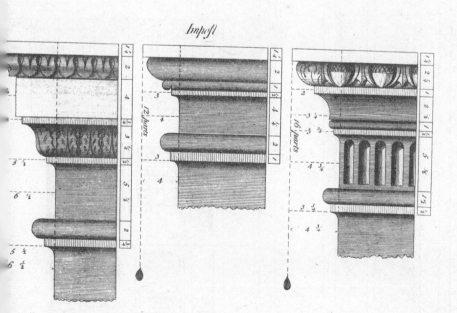

12 parts

16 parts

Four designs for Impost mouldings

Four Designs for Base & Surbase Mouldings

Fig A.

Fig B.

42

the breadth of Modillion 10 part, the distance 25 part, the Interval from Center to Center 35 part,

43

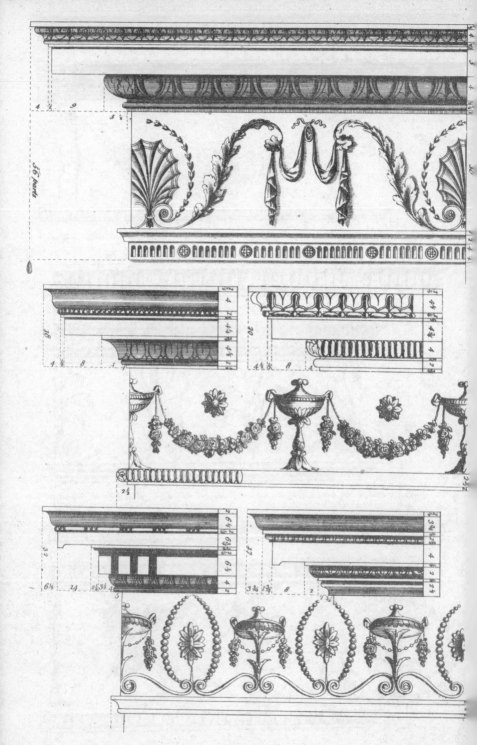

56 parts

44

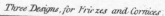

Russell sculp.

To Proportion the Frieze and Cornices, See fee Pl 50.

46

31 To proportion these Cornices with the frize & necking, give them ¾ of an Inch to a foot, including the frize &

Necking divide the whole into 12 parts give 5 to the Cornices & 6 to the frize 1 to the Neck moulding as Scale A.B.

48

Four Designs for Friezes.

*Vine leaves and Grapes dropt from a Pine for
the face of a Pilaster or any place required*

*Oak leaves &
acorns dropt
from a lions
Mask for a
Pilaster*

One fourth of a Ceiling

54

55

Ceiling to Dining Room

12   24   36   18

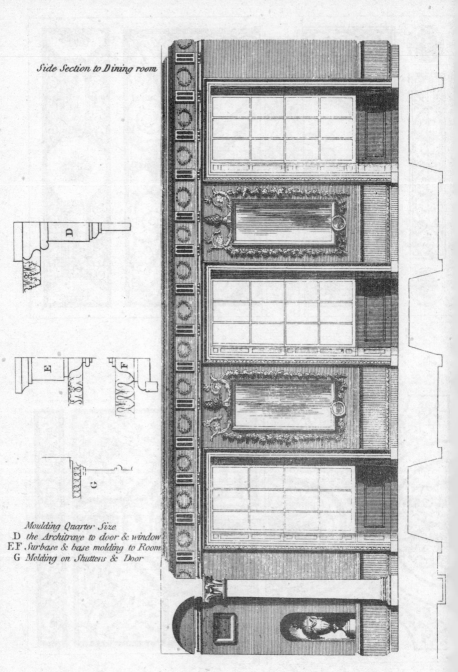

Side Section to Dining room

Moulding Quarter Size.
D *the Architrave to door & window*
E.F *Surbase & base molding to Room*
G *Molding on Shutters & Door*

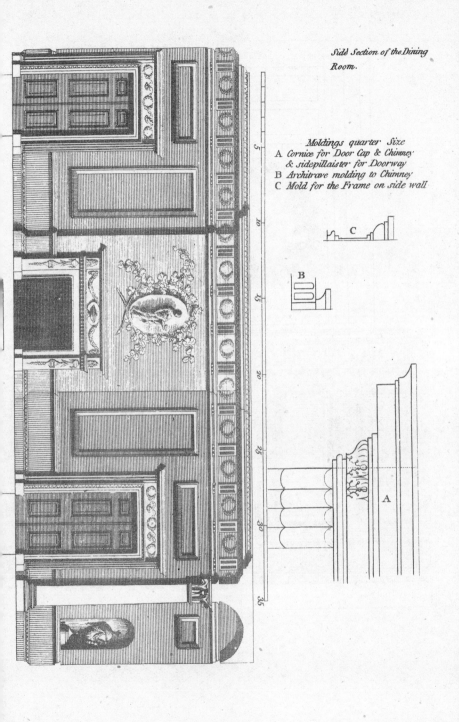

Side Section of the Dining Room.

Moldings quarter Size
A Cornice for Door Cap & Chimney
  & sidepillaister for Doorway
B Architrave molding to Chimney
C Mold for the Frame on side wall

C

B

A

5

10

15

20

25

30

35

End Section of the Dining room

Cornice & Frize round the Room
Quarter Size

60

A *The Base of Column & Pillaster*
B *The Nicking*
  Quarter Size

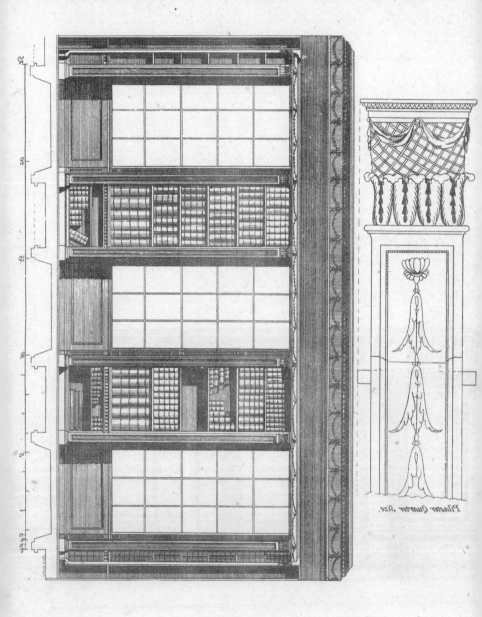

Pilaster Quarter Size.

62

A Surbase Mold quarter size
B Base Mold ditto
C Front Mold of Shelves to Bookcase

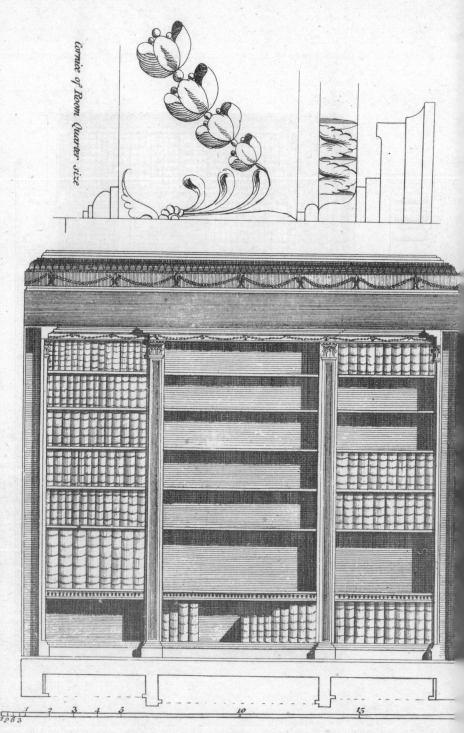

Cornice of Room Quarter size

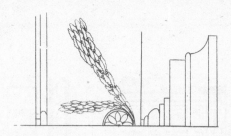

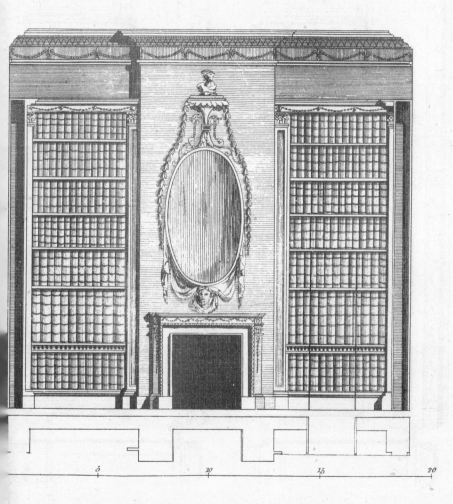

65

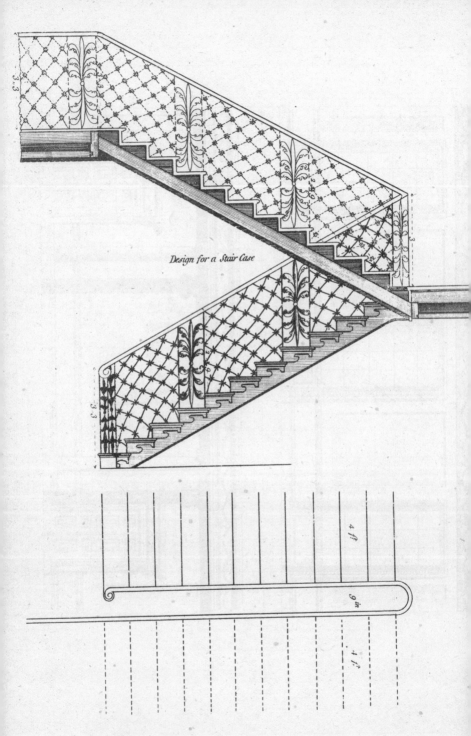

Design for a Stair Case

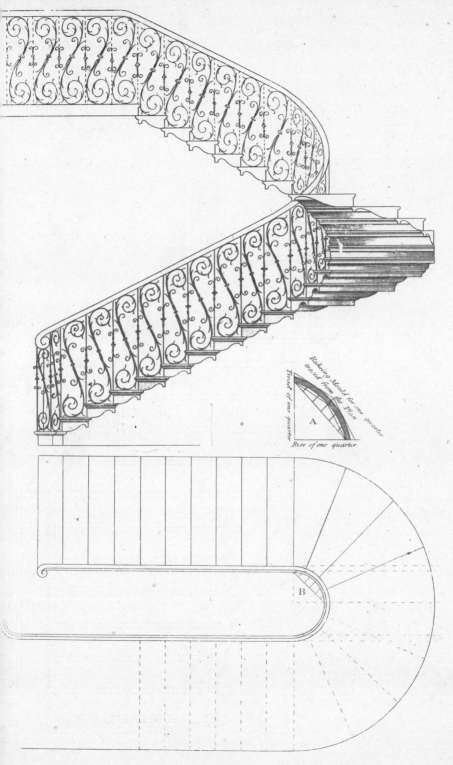

Raking Mould for one quarter
traced from the Plan

Tread of one quarter

A

Rise of one quarter

B

69

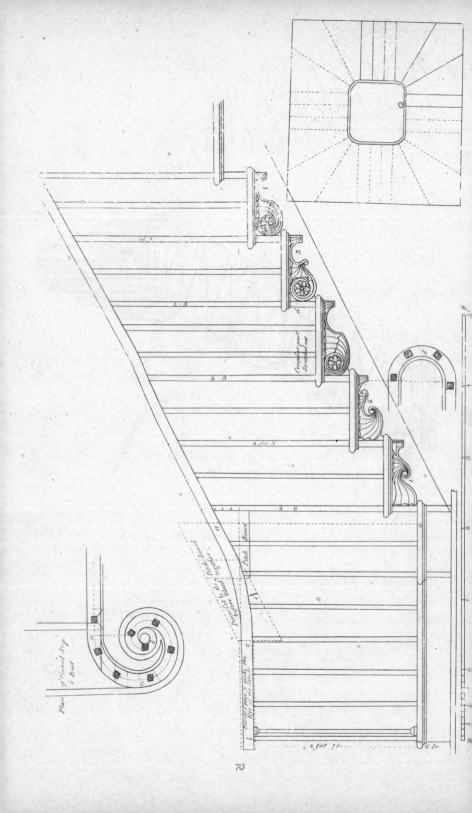

Circular part Stretched out

Pitch Board

Pitch Board

Pieces Cut by the Glued together

Straight paper to make the Eye of the Scrole

Plan of Curtail Step & Knit

2 feet 7 In

6 In

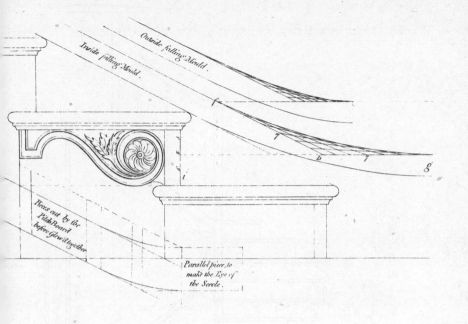

Outside filling Mould

Inside filling Mould

Pieces cut by the
Pitch Board
before Glew it together

Parallel piece, to
make the Eye of
the Scrole.

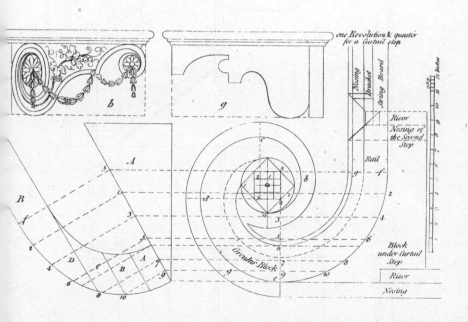

one Revolution & quarter
for a Curtail step

String Board
Bracket
Nosing

Risor
Nosing of
the Second
Step

Rail

A

B

Circular Block

Block
under Curtail
Step

Risor

Nosing

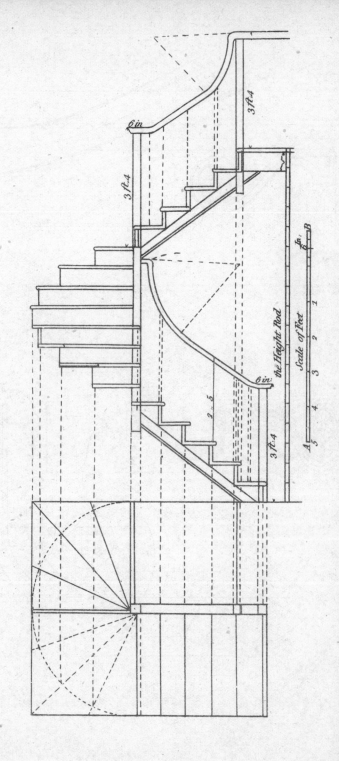

Common Flight of Stair: Close String and two quarter winders drawn by a Scale three Eights of an Inch to a Foot, the Step 9 In. one Inch rising.

6 in

3 ft 4

3 ft 4

6 in

2.5

3 ft 4

6 in

the Height Rod

Scale of Feet

5 4 3 2 1

A

B

In.
6

72

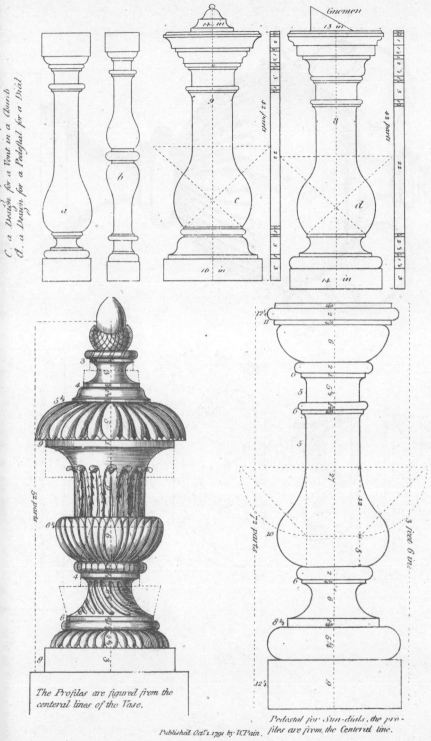

C, a Design for a Vont in a Church
D, a Design for a Pedestal for a Dial

Gnomen

Gnomen

The Profiles are figured from the
central lines of the Vase.

Pedestal for Sun-dials, the profiles are from the Central line.

Published Oct.ʳ 1. 1791 by W. Pain.

73

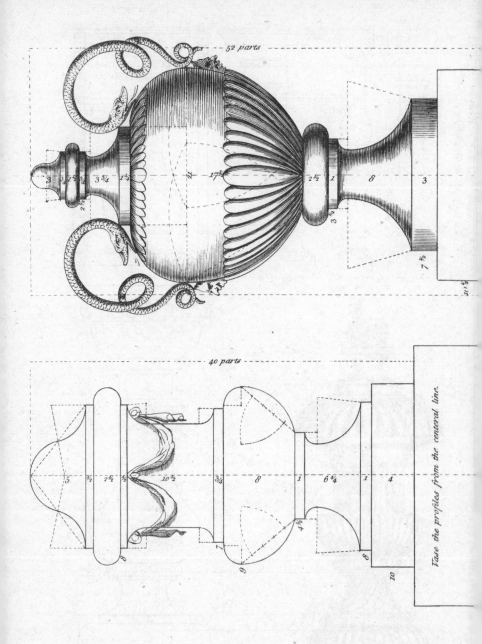

52 parts

3 · 1¾ 3½ · 3¾ · 1¼ · 4 · 17½ · 2½ 1 · 8 · 3

2½ · 3½ · 7½

40 parts

5 · 3½ · 2½ · ½ · 10½ · 3¼ · 8 · 1 · 6¼ · 1 · 4

8 · 7 · 9 · 4½ · 8 · 10

Vase the profiles from the central line.

74

NB. Any of the Cornices in this Book may be used to the Shop Fronts, divide the height here figured into as many parts as figured in the Cornice you make use of, and dispose them in the Moulding in height and projection as figured.

Front and profile of Columns & Pilasters for Shop Fronts

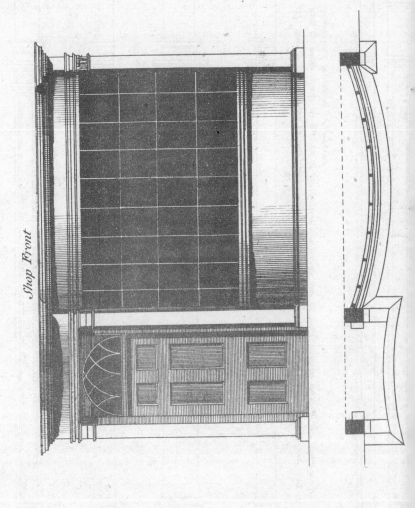

Shop Front

Shop Front

77

Shop Front